LISTEN UP, CLASS! PLEASE WELCOME NOH-A JOO TO AMITYVILLE PRIVATE HIGH SCHOOL.

SHE JUST TRANSFERRED TO THE NORTH DISTRICT, SO PLAY NICE!

TH-THERE'S SOMETHING FISHY ABOUT THIS CLASS.
AH~ I CAN ALREADY TELL YOU'LL BE THE BEST OF FRIENDS.
NOW, YOU NEED A SEAT...
....
NOH-A, TAKE THE SPARE SEAT BY THE WINDOW.
QUIT STARING AT ME, WILL YA?!
UGH...
...!

JACK FROST

The Amityville

VIOLENCE 1. AMITYVILLE

!!
파당
KWADANG (OOMPH)
EEEEK!!
OHHH~.
OUCH~. I-I'M SORRY. I WAS JUST... UM...
ZOMBIE MUCH? OR MAYBE HE'S JUST TRYING TO SAY "HI"? THEN I SHOULD TOO...
DID HE JUST SMILE AT ME? EWW. THAT'S SO CREEPY!
UM...H-HELLO?

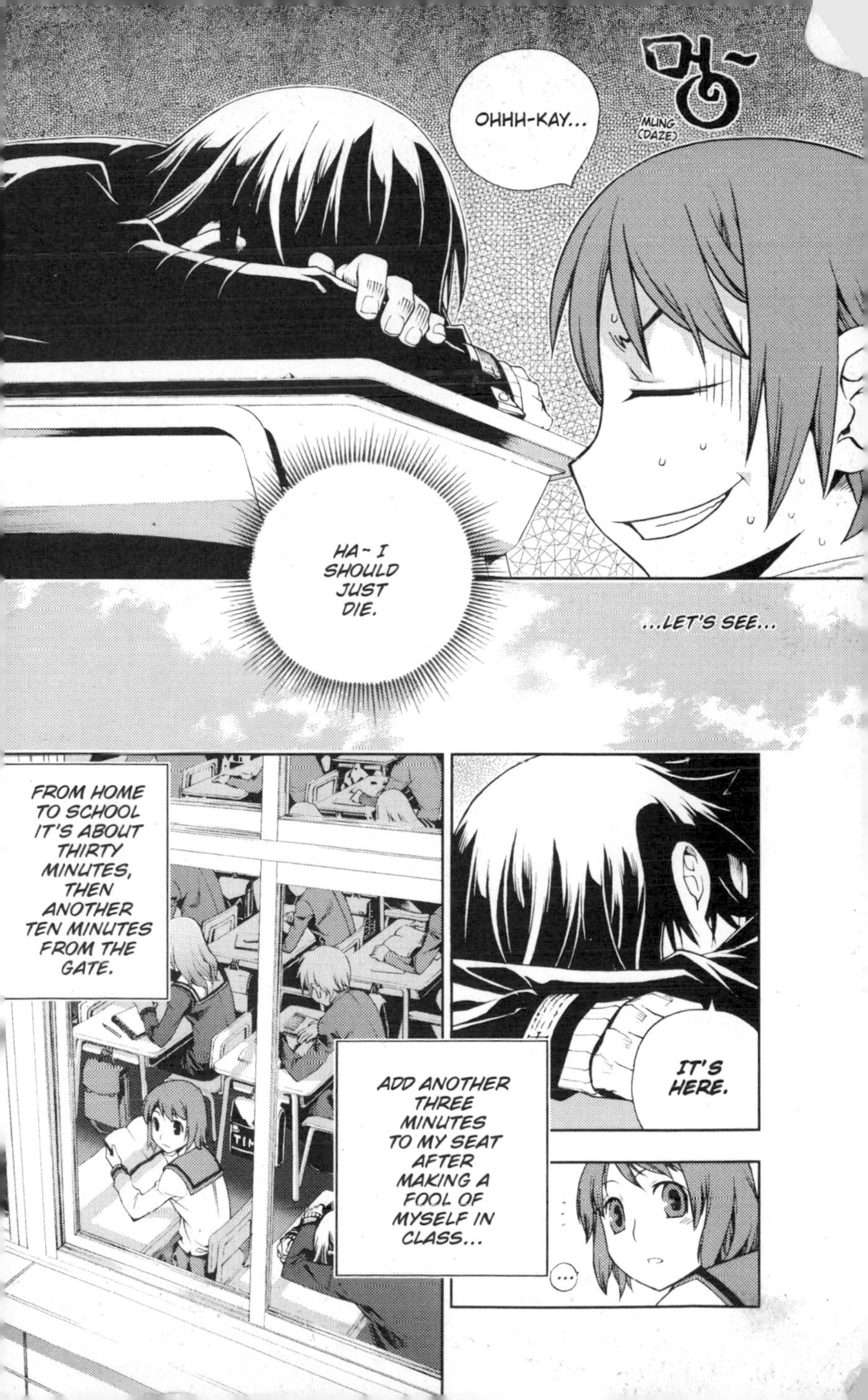
MUNG (DAZE)
OHHH-KAY...
HA~ I SHOULD JUST DIE.
...LET'S SEE...
FROM HOME TO SCHOOL IT'S ABOUT THIRTY MINUTES, THEN ANOTHER TEN MINUTES FROM THE GATE.
IT'S HERE.
ADD ANOTHER THREE MINUTES TO MY SEAT AFTER MAKING A FOOL OF MYSELF IN CLASS...
...

THEN TWO SECONDS LATER...
CHWAAK (SWISH)
AH...!

I REALLY DIED.

뻐억
BBUEK
(PACHAK)
퍼퍽퍽
PUPUPUK
(SHP)

쉬이이
SHIIII (SKKRESHHH)
THAT HIDEOUS, NASTY SMILE...?!
빠직
BBASIK (CRRECK)
KWANG (THUMP)
쾅
PINGRRRRR (SPIN)
핑그르르...
...!
WHUH-OAH!! NOT COOL!

I JUST BANGED MY HEAD PRETTY HARD. SHOULD I BE IN PAIN?
I GUESS I'LL DIE SOON ANYWAY. STILL, TO SEE ALL MY BLOOD SPATTERED EVERYWHERE IS TOTALLY GROSSING ME OUT.
HEH-HEH...
SSS (PHWIP)
THE LAST SURVIVOR IN THE NORTH DISTRICT?!
PFFT! A NEW KID.
YOU JERK, NASTY SMILE~. I NEED TO CHECK OUT YOUR FACE EVEN IF IT'S THE LAST THING I DO!
흔들
HUNDLE (WOBBLE)
흔들
HUNDLE

SHAAAA (VOOSH)
YO, THIS IS FUN AND ALL, BUT YOU SHOULD BE MORE CAREFUL.
KUOOHHH (SCHOOM)
YOU DON'T WANT TO END UP DEAD, DO YOU?

SO, FAITHFUL DOG OF CAMILLA FROM THE WEST DISTRICT...
...ALLOW ME TO WELCOME YOU TO THE NORTH DISTRICT!!
SHHHHUU (SHHUUUM)
......
NASTY SMILE'S MAKING THE STUDENTS DISAPPEAR?!
I KNEW IT! THE STUDENTS WERE A BARRIER!
CHZZZZ (ZZZZZTT)

ZZZZNG
(ZOOOM)
NO, NO~.

철컥
CHULKUCK (KA-CHAK)
THE NAME'S HANSEN. HEAD GUIDANCE COUNSELOR!
BY FINISHING YOU, I CAN ADD ANOTHER KILL TO MY RECORD.
AND THEN, THE WEST DISTRICT WILL TAKE OVER THE NORTH!
YOUR PRETTY LITTLE BOSS WILL JUST WET HER PANTS!
I BET SHE TASTES SWEET, HUH? HEH-HEH-HEH.
HEH...
HEH...
... HEH HEH!

ARGH... GRRRR... RARF RARF!
HEH!
CHAKANG (KACHING)
!!
YOU...
... BASTARD!
...!
"R-RARF"?! D-DID HE JUST BARK?!
KWAAK (CRACK)
HE'S FAST!
TA (BLAM)
TA
TANG
DIE!!

—THE HELL'S ON HIS ARMS?
OHSSA
(SHUDDE
KAGAGAK
(SKREEK)
!!
KANG
(KLANG)
CHWAAK
(SKREEE)
!
CHUK
(KA-CHAK)
DAMN...!!

WHAAA?! A FLYING LEG?!
WH ...!
WAAARRRGH!!
TA (BLAM)
TA
TANG

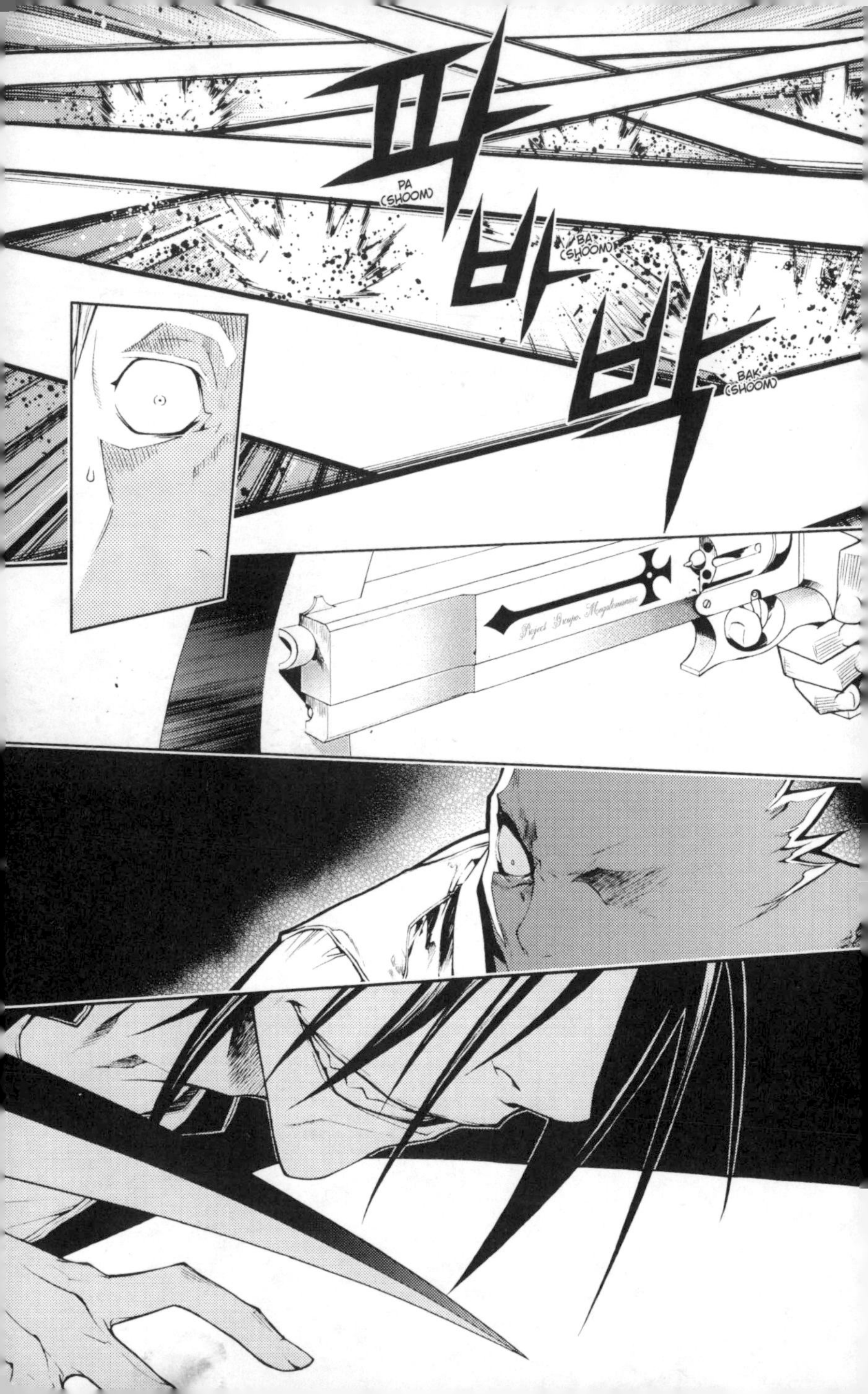
파
PA
(SHOOM)
바
BA
(SHOOM)
박
BAK
(SHOOM)

CHWAA
(SHLOOP)
UAAAHHH!!!
...
OUCH. THAT'S GOTTA HURT.

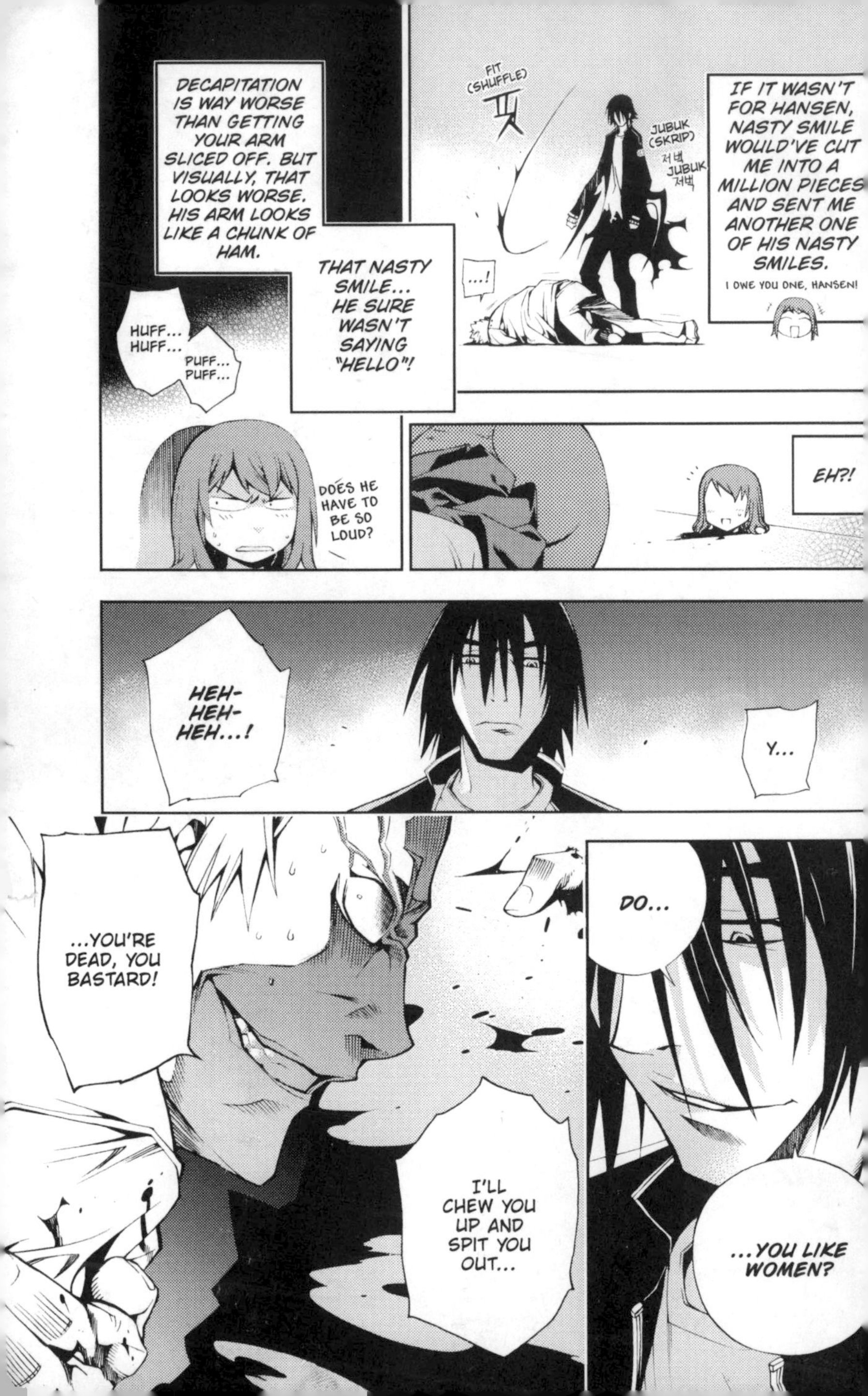
IF IT WASN'T FOR HANSEN, NASTY SMILE WOULD'VE CUT ME INTO A MILLION PIECES AND SENT ME ANOTHER ONE OF HIS NASTY SMILES.
I OWE YOU ONE, HANSEN!
JUBUK (SKRIP)
저벅
JUBUK
저벅
FIT (SHUFFLE)
픽
...!
DECAPITATION IS WAY WORSE THAN GETTING YOUR ARM SLICED OFF. BUT VISUALLY, THAT LOOKS WORSE. HIS ARM LOOKS LIKE A CHUNK OF HAM.
THAT NASTY SMILE... HE SURE WASN'T SAYING "HELLO"!
HUFF... HUFF...
PUFF... PUFF...
EH?!
DOES HE HAVE TO BE SO LOUD?
Y...
HEH-HEH-HEH...!
DO...
...YOU LIKE WOMEN?
...YOU'RE DEAD, YOU BASTARD!
I'LL CHEW YOU UP AND SPIT YOU OUT...

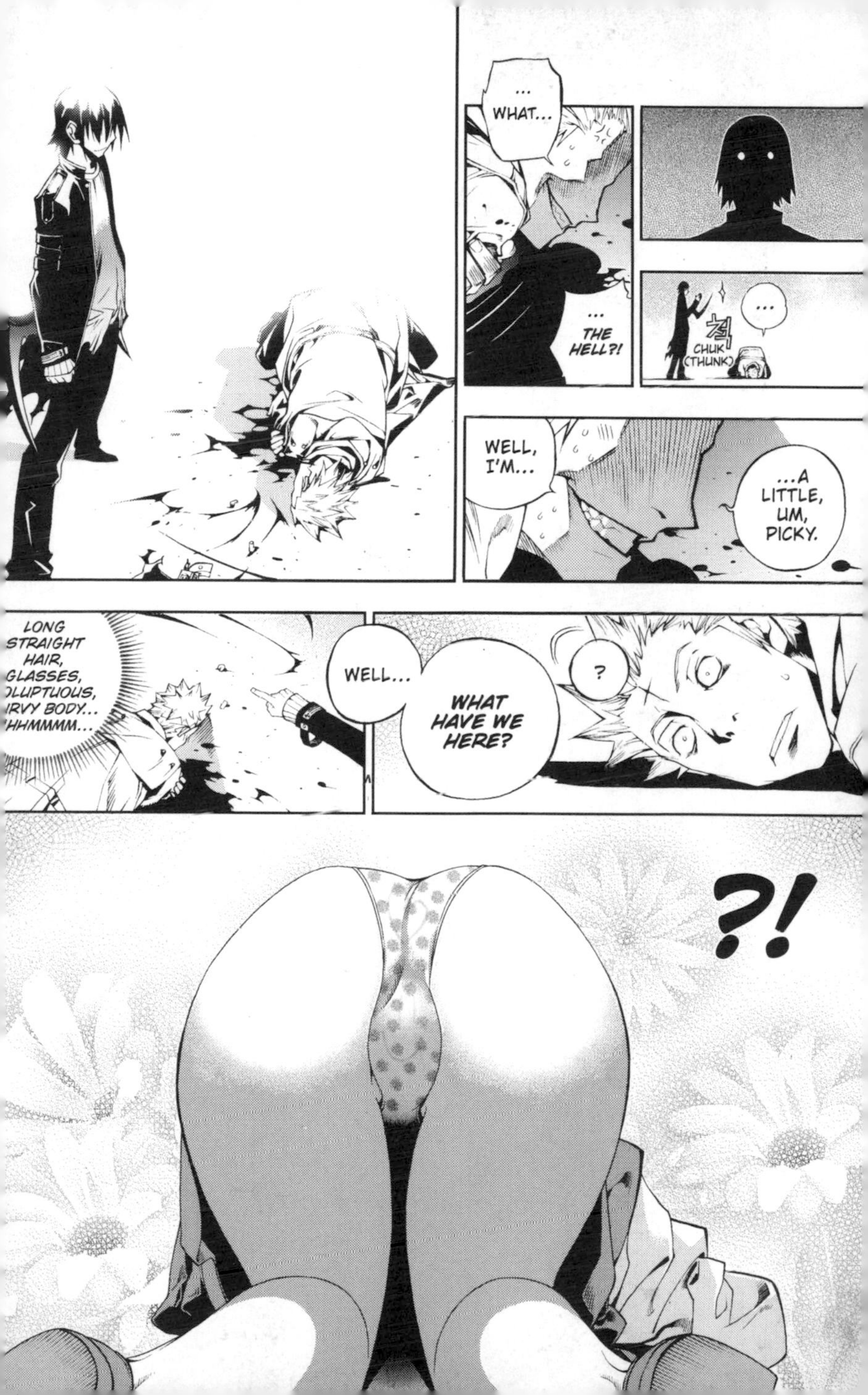
... WHAT...
... THE HELL?!
...
척
CHUK (THUNK)
WELL, I'M...
...A LITTLE, UM, PICKY.
?
WELL...
WHAT HAVE WE HERE?
LONG STRAIGHT HAIR, GLASSES, OLUPTUOUS, IRVY BODY... HHMMMM...
?!

THINK OF IT AS MY GIFT TO A DYING MAN...
T-THANK YOU.
...!
UGH!
HUNDLE (WOBBLE)
흔들
HUNDLE
흔들
WHAT?! HUH?! HOW? ISN'T THAT MY BODY? AND THAT POSE? SHE'S PRACTICALLY BEGGING FOR IT!
OH, HELL NO! THAT'S DISGUST-ING!!
!!
WHAT THE—! S-SHE'S STILL ALIVE?!
HOLD ON. THERE'S A BARRIER IN THIS CLASS-ROOM... SO HOW?!
EH?!

YUP, IT'S...
...A SPECIAL "MIRROR IMAGE"!
IT'S TIME TO DIE.
SSK
M-MIRROR IMAGE? WHAT'S THAT?
GOOD OR BAD, LUCK HAS NOTHING TO DO WITH WHY I CAN SEE MY HIPS PERFECTLY ANGLED LIKE THIS.
THOSE PATTERNED PANTIES ARE MY ULTRA COLLECTIBLE NO.1 PAIR!

THOSE TWO GUYS DIDN'T HAVE THIS BLOODFEST BY CHOICE.
WH- WHOA! H-HOLD ON!
IT'S ALL A DREAM ORCHESTRATED BY MY OWN CRAZY IMAGINATION.
EVER SINCE I STARTED HIGH SCHOOL, THE "TWO GUYS AND MY ULTRA COLLECTIBLE NO.1 PANTIES" DREAM HAS BEEN PART OF MY LIFE.
THE THING I DON'T GET IS THAT I NEVER SEE NASTY SMILE'S FACE. IF SOMEBODY TOLD ME I'D HAD MORE THAN ENOUGH CHANCES TO CATCH A GLIMPSE BY THIS POINT, I'D SAY THAT PERSON DIDN'T KNOW WHAT IT'S LIKE TO HAVE A DREAM.
HERE COMES THE LAST SCENE.
I JUST HAVE TO CLOSE MY EYES...
...AND IT WILL ALL BE OVER.
AH! AND THERE AREN'T ANY CLOSING CREDITS.

샤아아아...
SHAAAA (SSHHHHH)
KYAA~!
......
WHAT?!
KYAA? NOT YAWN?!
...

......
W-WHAT'S GOING ON ...?!
쿵 KUNG (BANG)
OH MY!
...
HEY.
DID YOU ENJOY YOUR NAP?

NOW, THIS MADE NO SENSE AT ALL!
THE "TWO GUYS AND MY ULTRA COLLECTIBLE NO.1 PANTIES" DREAM STARTED TO EVOLVE.
BEFORE I COULD DECIDE IF I SHOULD BE HAPPY OR WORRIED, I REALIZED I GOT SOMETHING OUT OF IT...

I FINALLY SAW NASTY SMILE'S FACE...
...HERE, IN AMITYVILLE!

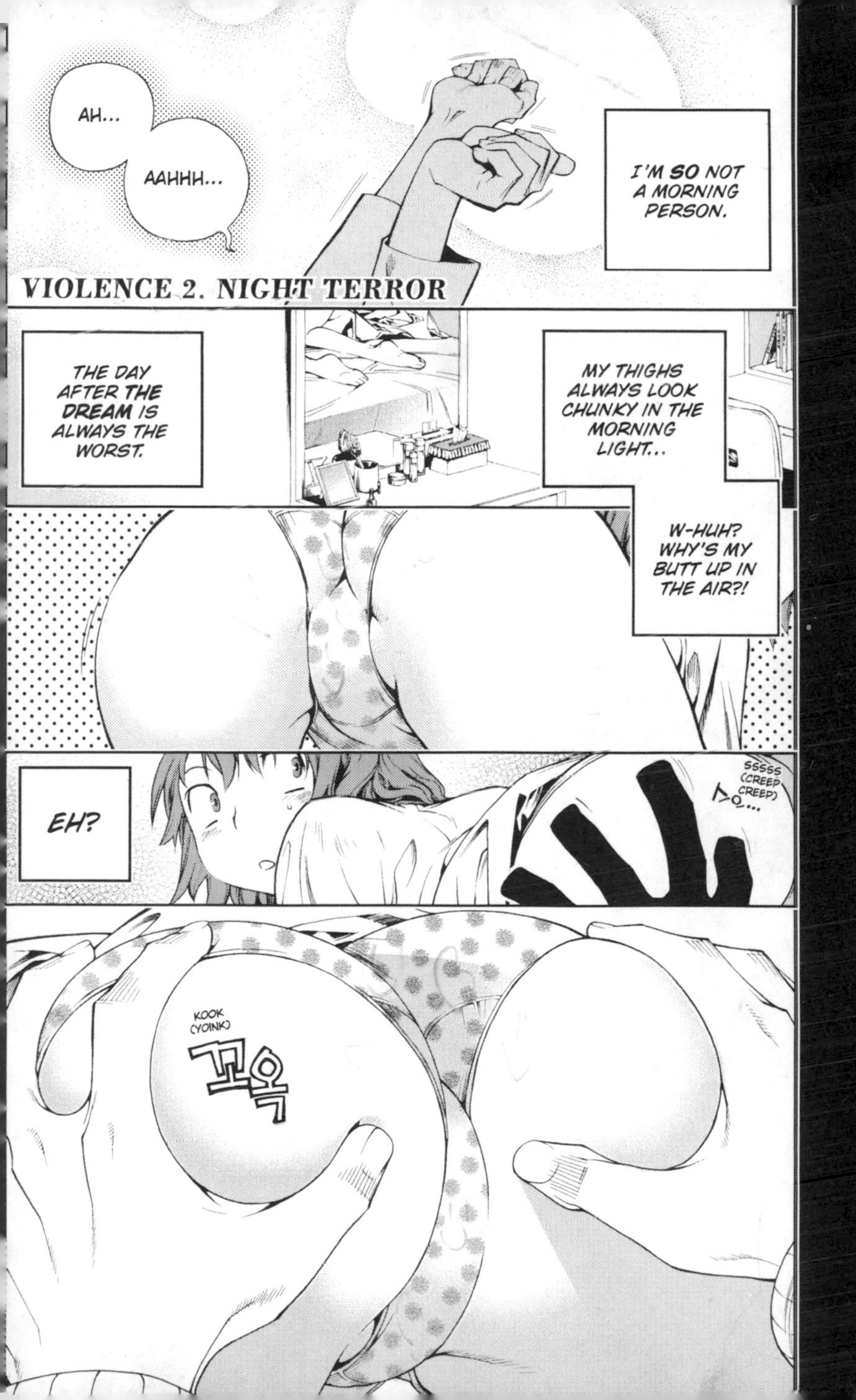
AH...
AAHHH...
I'M SO NOT A MORNING PERSON.
VIOLENCE 2. NIGHT TERROR
THE DAY AFTER THE DREAM IS ALWAYS THE WORST.
MY THIGHS ALWAYS LOOK CHUNKY IN THE MORNING LIGHT...
W-HUH? WHY'S MY BUTT UP IN THE AIR?!
EH?
SSSSS (CREEP CREEP)
KOOK (YOINK)

......!
NA ...!
콩!
KUNG (BONG)
WHAAAH —!!
KRRRR (SQUEEZE)

...NASTY SMILE!!!
JACK FROST
The Amityville
VIOLENCE 2.
NIGHT TERROR

HOW IS SHE DOING?
SHE'S STILL ALIVE...
...SHE'S THE MIRROR IMAGE, AFTER ALL.
OKAY.
I MUST MEET WITH THE DISTRICT HEAD.
WELL, LET'S LINK HER SEPARATE PARTS FIRST.
YES, SIR.
......

M-MY NECK?
WHAT'S GOING ON HERE...?
WHERE...?
?
ALREADY AWAKE?
MY, YOU HAVE QUITE THE QUICK RECUPERATIVE ABILITY, AS EXPECTED...
...MISS NOH-A JOO.
......

WHAA~!
I USED ALL MY POWER TO LINK YOUR SEVERED PARTS.
I'M STILL STUCK IN A GIRL'S WET DREAM?!
......
WOW~, SHE'S PRETTY HOT! SO COOL~.♡
YOUR NECK NEEDS ANOTHER HOUR TO HEAL.
BUT YOU SHOULD REGAIN YOUR FULL RANGE OF MOTION BY TOMORROW.
......
EX...
EH? MY VOICE IS BACK!
E-EX-CUSE...
...ME.
YES.
D'YOU MEAN YOU REATTACHED MY HEAD TO MY BODY?

JUST DOING MY JOB. MASTER "JACK" BROUGHT BOTH YOU AND THE WEST DISTRICT'S GUIDANCE COUNSELOR HERE.
YOU WERE UNCONSCIOUS, SO I HAD TO OPERATE ON YOU WITHOUT YOUR APPROVAL. I APOLOGIZE.
D'OH! OBVIOUSLY! STUPID QUESTION!
"NASTY SMILE" GUY? HE'S A "MASTER"...? REALLY?
N-NO PROBLEM. I SHOULD BE THANKING YOU.
CAN I ASK... WHERE EXACTLY ARE WE?

THE NORTH DISTRICT OF AMITYVILLE PRIVATE HIGH SCHOOL. THIS IS THE INFIRMARY.
MY NAME IS JIN. I'M IN CHARGE HERE.
THE NORTH DISTRICT OF AMITYVILLE PRIVATE HIGH SCHOOL?! COULD THAT NAME BE ANY LONGER?

NOW, WHAT I'M ABOUT TO TELL YOU MAY BE HARD TO BELIEVE.
I'M GUESSING YOU CAN TELL THIS SPACE ISN'T WHERE YOU USED TO LIVE.
BUT YOU MUST LISTEN CAREFULLY. OKAY?
......
SHE'S SO INTENSE... MAKES ME NERVOUS.

THE WEST DISTRICT KNOWS OF THE MIRROR IMAGE. SOON, SO WILL THE EAST AND SOUTH.
THEY'LL DEFY US AND TRY TO UNIFY AMITYVILLE...
EVER SINCE AMITYVILLE OPENED, THE EFFECTS OF KARMA COULD BE FELT. THEY WOULD START AND END CONTINUOUSLY.
THE EMERGENCE OF THE MIRROR IMAGE SIGNALS THE BEGINNING.
...DESPITE YOUR PRESENCE HERE, THE MOST POWERFUL IN AMITYVILLE, "JACK FROST"!

THEY WANT A FIGHT...?
BRING IT ON!!
I CAN ALREADY SMELL THEIR BLOOD.
....
NOW, NOW. DON'T GET TOO EXCITED...
...JACK.
HOW CAN I NOT? I'VE BEEN ALONE FOR SO LONG.
IT'S ABOUT TIME I HAD SOME CLASSMATES, AND A NORMAL "SCHOOL LIFE" HERE IN THE NORTH DISTRICT.
TRUE.

AND HOW'S...
...OUR YOUNG "MIRROR IMAGE" GIRL?
SHE'LL BE FINE IN A DAY. JIN'S TAKING CARE OF HER.
......
HMM. NOH-A JOO, WAS IT? DOES SHE KNOW...
...THAT, IN HER WORLD, SHE'S ALREADY DEAD?

SO WHAT?
WHETHER SHE LIVES OR DIES... WHO CARES?!
SHE'S IN AMITYVILLE NOW. THE MIRROR IMAGE IS OURS TO USE, RIGHT?
IT'S BEEN A FEW HUNDRED YEARS SINCE WE'VE HAD A MIRROR IMAGE. TREAT HER LIKE A LOVER, BE GENTLE...
THE GIRL'S JUST A "TOOL." A KEY.
I'M NOT GONNA PLEASE HER.

A TOOL IS A TOOL.
HER ONLY CONCERN SHOULD BE DOING MY "HOMEWORK"!
THAT'S SO YOU, JACK.

ZZZK (CREAK)
EVEN FALLEN TREES FLOWER LONG AFTER THEIR DEATHS. BUT YOU NEVER CHANGE.
YOU KILL AND KILL AGAIN, AND THEN YOU SMILE.
BECAUSE OF YOU, MY LEISURELY PASTIME ENDURES...
I'VE ALWAYS APPRECIATED YOUR SINCERITY.

...AND I CAN FOREVER GROW BEAUTIFUL FLOWERS...
...ON THE GRAVES OF THE FALLEN STUDENTS OF THE THIRTEEN AMITYVILLE WARS!

ARE YOU HAPPY...
...HELMINA?
......
SHWAAAA (WHOOSH)
쏴아아아
THE LAW OF CAUSALITY...
THE PRINCIPLE OF FLOW.
I'M DONE WITH OBSERVATION.
ONCE AGAIN...
SHHHSHHH

HEH-HEH-HEH...!
...NORTH DISTRICT, GET READY TO IMPOSE ORDER IN AMITYVILLE!!
I'VE WAITED A LONG TIME TO HEAR YOU SAY THAT, HELMINA, HEAD OF THE NORTH DISTRICT!
IT'S MUSIC TO MY EARS! HA-HA-HA!!
HEH-HA-HA-HA-HA!!

HA HA!
SERIOUSLY.
HA HA!!
SHUT UP, JACK!
HA-HA ...!
HA-HA-HA!
WHAAA?!
HUMANS WHO DIE GO TO THE WORLD OF THE DEAD.
I'M SORRY, BUT IT'S TRUE. YOUR LIFE IN THAT OTHER WORLD IS OVER.
SINCE YOU'VE ALREADY DIED ONCE, YOU NOW HAVE ETERNAL LIFE!
BUT YOU, MISS NOH-A JOO, ARE SPECIAL. YOU CAME TO "AMITYVILLE."
E-ETERNAL L-LIFE?!

AND THAT'S WHAT WE CALL THE "MIRROR IMAGE"!
TH-THIS HAS GOT TO BE...
M-MIRROR IMAGE?!
CONFUSING, I KNOW. YOU BETTER GET USED TO LIFE HERE. REST UP NOW.
A MIRROR IMAGE? ETERNAL LIFE?? I CAN GET USED TO THIS!! SWEET!!
...THE ULTRA COOLEST THING EVER!!
ジャーン
JJAN (TA-DAA)

AH!
I CAN MOVE!
I SEE YOU'VE REGAINED SOME MOBILITY.
......
THAT'S WHAT MAKES THE MIRROR IMAGE SO AMAZING.
OKAY, SO I REALIZE THIS ISN'T A DREAM, AND I'M DEAD AND ALL...
UM...
...CAN I ASK YOU A FAVOR?
EH?
코아악
KWAAK (GRAB)
NOTHING SPECIAL... JUST SOMETHING TO EAT, MAYBE?
참울
CHIMWOOL (GLOOMY)
WHAT'S THE FAVOR?
꼬르륵
KORRRK (RUMBLE)

콰
KRA-
앙
KWA-
(CHANG)
HUP!
탁
TAK

BWA-HA...!
하아 HUFF
하아 HUFF
ONLY TWO LITTLE GIRLS IN AN INFIRMARY? THIS'LL BE EASY!
ACK! H-HANSEN!!
HAS THIS DANGEROUS GUY BEEN HERE THE WHOLE TIME?!
HANSEN, HEAD GUIDANCE COUNSELOR OF THE WEST DISTRICT.
AS I THOUGHT, YOU HEALED UNUSUALLY QUICKLY.
...
US. RUN. NOW!!
IT'S A PITY YOU GIRLS WEREN'T BORN WITH LONG, STRAIGHT HAIR, GLASSES, AND VOLUPTUOUS CURVES.
PERHAPS I MIGHT'VE SPARED YOUR LIVES.

MY ARM! IT'S HEALED?!
...!
곰지락
KOMJIRA
(SQUIRM
KOMJIRA
B-BUT HOW?!
......
ISN'T SHE THE MIRROR IMAGE OR SOMETHING?
?!
ARGH! IS MY BLOOD LIKE GLUE OR SOMETHING?
HAERONG (WOOZY) HAERONG
AH...I'M GONNA FAINT~.
I USED HER BLOOD TO SAVE YOUR ARM.
YOU HAVE MISS NOH-A TO THANK FOR THAT.
EH?
OH YEAH. THE FAMOUS ETERNAL MIRROR IMAGE! I THOUGHT IT WAS A LOAD OF CRAP, BUT MY ARM WAS SLICED CLEAN OFF. AND LOOK AT IT NOW!

YOUR EYES DON'T DECEIVE YOU, PUNK!
YOU'RE LATE.
SSS (PAT PAT)
?
YIPES...?!
AH, SHE TOOK LONGER THAN EXPECTED.
I- IT'S...
...IT'S YOU!!
IT'S NASTY SMILE! WHAT'S HIS NAME? JACK?
'BOUT TIME YOU SHOWED UP!

YOU SNEAKY BASTARD —!!
PFFT!
KHWAJAC
CKRA-CHUD

BZZT
BZZT
DAMMIT!
W-
WHAT?!
MPHLB!
HAVING
FUN
YET?
TUD
(GRAB)
THIS IS
FUN!
TOOKWAK
(WHA-CHUK)

ZZKUCK (CHUD)
......!
!!
KWA- (CRE-)
-JICK (C-EAK)
SO...?
WHO THE HELL IS HE?!

IS HE A MONSTER?
YOU HAD ENOUGH?!
KUOOOHHH (WHOOSH)

HEH-HEH-HEH...!
INJURED OR NOT, HANSEN COULD NEVER BEAT JACK!
JUST KILL ME! NOW!!
DON'T YOU HEAL ME AGAIN. I'D RATHER DIE TRYING TO EAT EVERY LAST ONE OF YOU! EVEN YOUR BONES!
......!
HOW SAD.

I'D LIKE YOU TO TRANSFER TO THE NORTH DISTRICT...
...HANSEN.
AH...
GLASSES... AND LONG HAIR...
...A VOLUPTUOUS BODY!
......

YOU WON'T GET ME WITH SUCH HYPNOTIC TRICKERY!
HOW-EVER...
I'LL LICK YOU TO DEATH. STARTING WITH YOUR TOES.
...I THINK I'LL DEFEAT YOU IN ANOTHER WAY.
FROM NOW ON, YOUR JOB WILL BE CLEANING AND GENERAL MAINTENANCE. GOT IT?
YES, MA'AM.
YOU CAN START WITH THE INFIRMARY. IT'S YOUR FAULT IT'S MESSED UP...
...
HALZACK (CLICK) HALZACK
할짝~ 할짝~
SULGUM (SHUFFLE) SULGUM
슬금 슬금
YES, MA'AAAM!
WHATEVER YOU SAY, MA'AAAM!
I THINK SHE LIKES IT!
WHO IS SHE ANYWAY?
THE HEAD OF NORTH DISTRICT, HELMINA.
A LITTLE PERVY, ISN'T SHE?
THERE IS NO EVIDENCE OF ANY PERVERTED BEHAVIOR BY THE HEAD OF THE NORTH DISTRICT.
...?
WHY'RE YOU TALKING LIKE THAT?
THERE IS NO ANSWER FOR THAT TYPE OF QUESTION.

JACK FROST
The Amityville
VIOLENCE 3. AVID
파창
PACHING (CLANG)

COME.

KWHA-
-CHANG

KA
(CLANG)
KA
KANG
PFFT!
PSHAW

PAKANG (CLANG)
PA (BOOM)
PA
PANG
CHEPAT (SHLOOP)

SHUPAAK
(SHHHHK)
HUH~.
THEY WEREN'T KIDDING WHEN THEY CALLED YOU THE "MOST POWERFUL MAN IN THE NORTH DISTRICT"!

AND WHAT ABOUT YOU, PUNK? HAVE A NAME?
SSIK (SNEER)
WHIIIIII (WHOOSH)
HEY~.
E-EXCUSE ME.
ANYBODY THERE?

BUT WHERE'S MY BODY THIS TIME? IF IT'S IN ANOTHER EROTIC POSE, SO HELP ME—
MY NECK IS SEVERED AGAIN~. THIS IS SO NOT COOL!
...
EH?
JIN! NO!!
I-IS SHE DEAD? NO~! MY ONLY FRIEND IN THIS PLACE.
WHAT KIND OF CLASS IS THIS? I HATE THIS SCHOOL!

TWO HOURS EARLIER IN AMITYVILLE NORTH DISTRICT.

쏴아 아아... SHWAAAA (WHOOSH)

I SO HATE SCHOOL.

TEACHERS CAN DENY IT, BUT IT JUST AIN'T FUN.

INDEPENDENT NIGHT CLASSES ARE SO BORING! IT'S SO EASY TO DRIFT OFF INTO DREAMLAND.

I'D LOVE THE POWER TO STOP TIME AND COPY ANSWERS FROM THE NERDS. OR TO READ PEOPLE'S MINDS TO SEE WHO THEY'RE CRUSHING ON!

...

IT'S NOT UNUSUAL FOR A GIRL TO DREAM SHE HAS SPECIAL ABILITIES.

BUT I WONDER...

...WHAT SHOULD A GIRL DO IF SHE BECOMES THAT "SPECIAL ME" AFTER DEATH?

LIKE ME, THE "MIRROR IMAGE."

ZZAP!

IN THE NAME OF THE MIRROR I WILL DEFEAT YOU*!

* PARODY OF SAILOR MOON.

MIRROR IMAGE POWER MAKEUP!
DEAR MIRROR, HELP ME SAVE THE POOR STUDENTS!
GO VOLT ATTACK! MIRROR-CHU* ~!
* PARODY OF CARTOON CHARACTER "PIKACHU."
DARKNESS BEYOND TWILIGHT, CRIMSON BEYOND BLOOD THAT FLOWS, BURIED IN THE FLOW OF TIME, IN THY GREAT NAME, HERE I MAKE A VOW TO A MIRROR**.
** PARODY OF CARTOON THE SLAYERS.
DA (TAK) DA DA
YEEEAAA~!
MIRROR SLAVE...
쿵
KUNG (BUMP)
CRAP!
OUCHIE...
EWWW!! NASTY SMILE!! I-I MEAN JACK!!
'THE HELL ARE YOU DOING?
...
'THE HELL ARE YOU DOING?
ENTERING A LADY'S ROOM WITHOUT PERMISSION? THE NERVE! STOP STARING!
슬금 슬금~
SULGUM (SHUFFLE) SULGUM
GET OUT~!

...
WHAAA?!
W-WHEN DID I...?!
KUNG (GOONG)
ARE YOU TRYING TO BE CUTE? OR ARE YOU REALLY *THAT* DUMB?
THIS IS A HALL.
ARGH- I WAS TOO EXCITED TO SEE I ENDED UP IN THE HALL! STUPID...STUPID...
IT'S YOUR OLD SCHOOL UNIFORM. YOU'RE A STUDENT HERE AT AMITYVILLE.
THIS IS...
GET RID OF THAT SHAPELESS BODY...
SH-SHAPE-LESS?
OH, I'VE GOT EVERY-THING I'M SUPPOSED TO HAVE!!
GET DRESSED, AND JIN WILL SHOW YOU AROUND.
ACK!
PAAK (THUD)

SNIFF~. I THOUGHT I'D GET SOME KIND OF SUPERHERO GEAR.
THIS OLD THING...
SARARAK (FLAP)
...
HERE, LET ME HELP.
SSRRRK
WHIIK (YANK)
AIEE! J-JIN~!
2-C
THIS IS A CLASSROOM WHERE STUDENTS STUDY.
WE'RE A CO-ED SCHOOL. MAXIMUM THIRTY PER CLASS.
...
THAT IS THE SECOND PLAYGROUND.
IT'S A GYMNASIUM FOR SPECIAL OCCASIONS OR WHEN IT RAINS.
OTHER THAN ITS DATED LOOK IT'S LIKE ANY OTHER SCHOOL.

THE NORTH DISTRICT OF AMITYVILLE PRIVATE HIGH CONSISTS OF THREE STUDENT BUILDINGS, A TEACHERS' BUILDING, AND STUDENT HOUSING.
EH? THERE'RE MORE BUILDINGS?
STUDENT BUILDINGS ARE THREE TIMES LARGER AND HAVE MORE FACILITIES THAN THE TEACHERS'. OTHER DISTRICTS ARE NOT ALLOWED IN.
THERE ARE MORE DISTRICTS?!
AMITYVILLE HAS FOUR DISTRICTS. WEST, EAST, SOUTH, AND NORTH. EACH DISTRICT IS RUN BY ITS OWN HEAD.
WOOOW! THREE MORE BIG SCHOOLS LIKE THIS?!
ACTUALLY, THE NORTH DISTRICT IS SMALLER THAN THE OTHERS.
...!
FOUR DISTRICTS COMBINED, AMITYVILLE PRIVATE HIGH SCHOOL IS AS LARGE AS A COUNTRY IN THE HUMAN WORLD.
U-UN-BELIEV-ABLE!
BUT WHERE ARE THE TEACHERS AND OTHER STUDENTS? I DON'T SEE ANYONE!

W-WHAT IS SHE TALKING ABOUT? IS A TEACHER LIKE A THING HERE?
THIS WAY IF YOU'D LIKE TO SEE THE TEACHERS.
W-
W-WAIT FOR ME~.
HMMM, TEACHERS ...
I BELIEVE WE HAVE SOMETHING LIKE THAT...
WHAT? SOMETHING LIKE THAT?!
HUK (HUFF) HUK
헉~
헉
NO. NOT YET.
A LITTLE BIT LONGER, HANSEN.
...
탁 탁 탁
TAK TAK TAK
M-MA'AM, ARE YOU NOT SATISFIED YET? I-I CAN'T...
SHOULD I RECONSIDER KEEPING SUCH A WEAK MAN LIKE YOU UNDERNEATH ME?
WHAT?
BUT...
I... CAN'T HOLD IT ANY MORE.

I'M SORRY, MA'AM! I DIDN'T THINK CLEANING WAS THIS HARD! I'LL DO ANYTHING ELSE?
HOW DISAPPOINTING, TRANSFER STUDENT! CAN'T EVEN CLEAN YOUR OWN MESS.
탁 탁 탁
TAK TAK TAK
I'M GOOD AT DESTROYING! NOT HOUSEHOLD CHORES!
SILENCE, BOY!
ZZIIK (TIGHT)
YIKES! SORRY, MA'AM!
ZZWAAK
SEE? TOTAL PERVERT.
I'LL ADD IT TO THE DATA.
ZZWAAK (WHIP)
HUFF HUFF
OH, HI. NOH-A.
ENJOYING THE TOUR OF THE SCHOOL?
Y-YES, MA'AM.
...
I'M ON THE WAY TO SEE THE TEACHERS WITH JIN.
슬금...
SULGUM (FLINCH)
슬금...
SULGUM
HMMM...
TEACHERS...
MA'AM.
FINE. I'LL TAKE IT FROM HERE.
COME ALONG, HANSEN.
Y-YES, MA'AM!
...

DRRRRK (SWISH)
AND HERE ARE THE TEACHERS.
OH~.
I-IT IS...
IT'S THE TEACHERS' LOUNGE IN THE NORTH DISTRICT OF AMITYVILLE.

IT HAPPENED A FEW HUNDRED YEARS AGO DURING THE FINAL ATTACK FROM ANOTHER DISTRICT.
THE TEACHERS HAD A MEETING AT THE TIME.
EVERY LIVING THING IN HERE BURNED. THEY WERE SO UNLUCKY.
OF COURSE, JACK KILLED THE ONE RESPONSIBLE. WE KEEP THE SCENE LIKE THIS AS A MEMORIAL OF THAT DAY.
ASIDE FROM JIN, NONE OF THE STAFF OR STUDENTS HAVE BEEN REPLACED.
WE CAN BARELY MAINTAIN THE SCHOOL WITH ITS CURRENT MEMBERS.
WHAT? THAT'S A TOTAL OF FIVE MEMBERS INCLUDING NASTY SMILE.
HMMM.
SO, LET'S FIND A REAL TROOPER WHO'LL WORK FOR THE SCHOOL 24/7! HERE WE GO!
SSS (CRUMBLE)

BUNJUK (FLASH)
SHUUUU (WHOOSH)
?!
CHU (KRZZT) CHU CHU
H-HOW?!
SHE REVIVED A CORPSE!
BRAVO~! I SEE WHY YOU'RE THE HEAD OF THE DISTRICT!
!
GET YOUR BROOM AND APRON!
HE'S THE CHIEF TEACHER.
KUMTLE (WRIGGLE)
KADDAK (MOVE)
AH~.
...!
HE KEPT THE SCHOOL CLEAN WHEN HE WAS ALIVE. LET HIM CONTINUE HIS JOB!
HERE'S YOUR NORTH DISTRICT UNIFORM AND YOUR GUN!
YESSS~! I THOUGHT I LOST MY GUN! AND NO MORE CLEANING!
COOL!
SHUT UP, USELESS BOY!
THANK YOU, MA'AM.
...
EXCUSE ME, I HAVE A QUESTION.

OKAY, SO I KNOW EACH DISTRICT IS FIGHTING FOR SOME REASON.
AND I'M THE SPECIAL "MIRROR IMAGE" AND HAVE ETERNAL LIFE.
BUT I'VE HEARD EACH STUDENT HERE HAS A SPECIAL ABILITY.
NOW, I *USED* TO BE AN ORDINARY SCHOOLGIRL. HEE-HEE.
IF I'M REALLY SO SPECIAL...
...WHAT IS MY SPECIAL POWER?
......
NOTHING.
OTHER THAN YOU CAN NEVER DIE, NOTHING.
......
PHYSICAL POWER: ZERO. MENTAL POWER: ZERO. PURE HUMAN. THAT'S YOU, MISS NOH-A JOO.
...
WHAT?!
I-IT CAN'T BE!
KAAAAA (ARGH)
I'VE DREAMT OF BEING A MAGICAL POWER GIRL! A SUPER-HERO!
HOWEVER, IT'S TRUE...

...THAT NEITHER MYSELF NOR JACK HAVE THE MOST IMPORTANT POWER IN ALL OF AMITYVILLE.
EH?
IT'S YOU, THE MIRROR IMAGE.
YOU'LL KNOW WHY SOON ENOUGH.
AH, WAIT...!
휙
WHIK (SWISH)
JUCHUM (FLINCH)
SO, THE MIRROR IMAGE IS IMPORTANT...
...NOT NOH-A JOO?
WAITAMINNIT... THAT MEANS NOH-A JOO ISN'T IMPORTANT, ONLY THAT SHE'S THE MIRROR IMAGE WITH ETERNAL LIFE!
...
LET ME GET THIS STRAIGHT. I HAVE NO ABILITIES AT ALL... EXCEPT FOR MY BLOOD. IT CAN REATTACH SEVERED LIMBS!
SAK (SWEEP)
삭
삭
SAK
PLEASE, PROTECT ME, MIRROR IMAGE.
IF I'M HURT, I'LL CALL YOU RIGHT AWAY.
NO! THEY'LL TREAT ME LIKE A GLUE-STICK OR SOMETHING! I MUST PROVE MY WORTH!
NOW, WHERE'S JACK?
WAIT! I'M A MASTER WITH INSTANT NOODLES!

TUDUDUK (RUMBLE)
KRA-
-KWAM
?!!

WHAT'S HAPPENING, JIN?!
WHAT THE?!
TATAK (TMP)
I'M SORRY. I'LL GO FIND OUT RIGHT NOW!
슈우우우...
SHOOOOOO
ARIDIO CE LUDINO PRETESS...
...
?
THAT'S THE LANGUAGE OF THE PIRATES.
CHAKANG (CLICK)
IT MEANS "MY BEAUTIFUL TREASURES"!
우우우...
WOOOOO

!!
I-IT'S YOU?!
......
YOU KNOW HIM?
PAAK (CH-UCK)
HE CALLS ANYTHING HE LIKES "TREASURE."
AND JUST LIKE A PIRATE, HE HUNTS FOR HIS TREASURE!
BLOOD PIRATE AVID!!
THE WORST BLOOD-SUCKING HUNTER OF THE SOUTH DISTRICT!
EH?
I'VE BEEN WAITING FOR YOU, YOU PERVERT!

!!
PAKWAK
(KA-POW)
UGH...
!
STRANGE. HAVE WE MET?
THE CROSS ON YOUR FOREHEAD...
AH~ I REMEMBER YOU.
THE "TASTELESS MEAL"! I ACCIDENTALLY SUCKED YOUR BLOOD.
부르르
BURURU
(SHIVER)

ZZEEEEK
(KOOOOM)
SHUPAAK
(PA-CHAK)

CHIGIGIK
(KRZZT)
HMPH!
I JUST HATE "LEFT-OVERS"!!
TOOK
(TAK)
DUGUN
(THROB)
PANG
(POW)
M-MA'AM...

휘이익
SHHHK (FWIP)
?!
퍼억
POOEK (WHOOMP)
쿠당탕
KUDANGTANG (THUD)
...!
CRAP...
DAMN IT.
I'M NO PUNCHING BAG!!
SIGH~.
DID I CUT IT TOO CLOSE?
NO.

JUDA GE BLEED...
NICE TO MEET YOU, MISS "MIRROR IMAGE."
BUT SHE'S STILL IN DANGER...
E-EXCUSE ME. I *THINK* HE'S GOT ME.

FIT
(SHLURP)
FIT
AH...
LET'S GO BACK TO A TEENAGE GIRL'S DREAM.
WHILE SHE DREAMS ABOUT THE "SPECIAL ME," SHE ALSO DREAMS...
...OF WHEN SHE FACES DARKNESS AND FEAR...
YOU...
Y-YOU...!
...THERE'S A PRINCE WHO SAVES THE GIRL FROM DANGER.
THE MAN...!

BUT PLEASE, ANYONE BUT "JACK FROST." HE'S GOT A TEMPER AND A NASTY SMILE!

DAD?
WHAT IS THIS?
A DOLL... A VERY GOOD DOLL.
HE'LL PROTECT YOU WHEN I NO LONGER CAN.
OH! WHAT'S ITS NAME?
VIOLENCE 4.
NIGHT OF CRESCENT

JACK...
JACK FROST.

JACK FROST
The Amityville

VIOLENCE 4.
NIGHT OF CRESCENT

WHAT JUST HAPPENED? WAS THAT A DREAM...? I CAN'T REMEMBER... I THINK I SAW SOMEONE.
UGH...
EH?
FOOL...
YOU CUT THE SECURITY SYSTEM OFF, DIDN'T YOU, JACK?
HEH HEH HEH...
OHH-KAY! BAD TIME FOR A DREAM!
SURE, HE WAS ABOUT TO SUCK HER BLOOD, BUT YOU DIDN'T HAVE TO CHOP OFF HER HEAD!
?!

I TRIED TO CUT YOU ALONG WITH THE HEAD OF THE MIRROR IMAGE!
SOMEHOW, YOU MANAGED TO AVOID IT!
C'MON!
AREN'T WE HAVING FUN YET?!
Y YOU...
YOU BASTARD!!
IS THAT JACK?
YOU ONE-EYED PUNK!
KOOUK (GRIP)
I LIKE YOU.

추욱
CHUOOK (HOIST)
TASTE IT! THE BLOOD OF THE MIRROR IMAGE!
IT'S STILL WARM!!
흠칫
HUMCHIT (FLINCH)
MIRROR IMAGE OR NOT...
TING (CLANG)
...IF YOU UNDER-STOOD THE BEAUTY OF VAM-PIRES...
IDIOT...
BURRRRR (SHUDDER)
EEK! THAT'S MY BODY!!
BBAJIK (GNASH)
빠직

CHWARARAK (SHLOOP)
...YOU'D NEVER OFFER ME A LIFELESS, UGLY BODY!
ZZEPAT (KRA-CHUD)
PAANG (WHEE-CHUK)
?!

TUDUDUK (RIP)
VAMPIRES...
SRRR (SLIDE)
OH~.
...ONLY FEAST ON LIVE BEAUTIES.
TULSUK (THUD)
THINGS THAT CAN'T RESIST...
...HAVE NO FLAVOR!
I SEE...
I'M IN TOTAL AGREEMENT!

샤샥
SHASHAK (SHP-SHP)
슈파악
SHUPAAK (PA-CHAK)

QUEQUE
(WHISH)
KOONG
(KROOOM)

THOSE TWO. INCREDIBLE.
I DON'T KNOW THE FIRST THING ABOUT FIGHTING, BUT WOW~!
I CAN TELL...
...THIS WILL BE A MOST INTERESTING "CLASS."
WHAA~?! YOU CALL THIS A CLASS?!
SHIIIII (SHANK)
EH?!
SHU- (SHO-)
-ONG (-OOP)
따악
DDAAK (WHACK)
KEK!

THE NORTH DISTRICT OF AMITYVILLE, PRESENT.

AND I FAINTED, JUST LIKE THAT.

WHEN I WOKE UP, IT WAS JUST ME AND JIN. I THOUGHT SHE WAS DEAD!
CRAP!
DAMN! MY IMPORTANCE... WAS IT ALL A LIE?
쨍그랑
ZANGGRANG (CLA-CLANK)
?!
W-WHAT WAS THAT? HELMINA? A CAT? PLEASE, JIN, IF YOU'RE ALIVE, WAKE UP!
흔들
HUNDLE (SHAKE)
흔들
HUNDLE
KE-KEK.
N-NO! I CAN'T SPEAK—I CAN'T EVEN MOVE! WHAT THE HELL'S GOING ON?! I'M SCARED. SOMEBODY, PLEASE, HELP!
쉬이이...
SHIIII (WHOOSH)
팍
PAK (FFT)

KUNG (THUMP)
SHUKWA (PA-CHAK)
INTERESTING. COMING OUT OF YOUR ARM, IS IT?
ROUGH AND SIMPLE, BUT SOMEHOW IT'S STILL BEAUTIFUL.
KANG
KANG
KANG (CLANG)

FIRST THE MIRROR IMAGE, AND NOW THIS ONE?!
DO YOU WANT ME TO PUT OUT YOUR OTHER EYE?!
CHA- (CLA-)
-ANG (-NG)
DO YOU KNOW...
...THE VALUE OF YOUR NAME IN AMITYVILLE?!
KUOOHHHH (WHOOSH)
JACK FROST!!
PING

TI-
(KERR-)
THE ONLY STUDENT TO SURVIVE ALL THE "CLASSES" IN AMITYVILLE... JACK FROST!
-KANG
(-RRANG!)
ZZPAT
(KRZZT)
TITIK
(TA-TAK)
FIT
(FFT)
FIT
THE LAST MAN STANDING IN THE NORTH DISTRICT AFTER THIRTEEN AMITYVILLE UNIFIED WARS, JACK FROST!
TITIKTIK

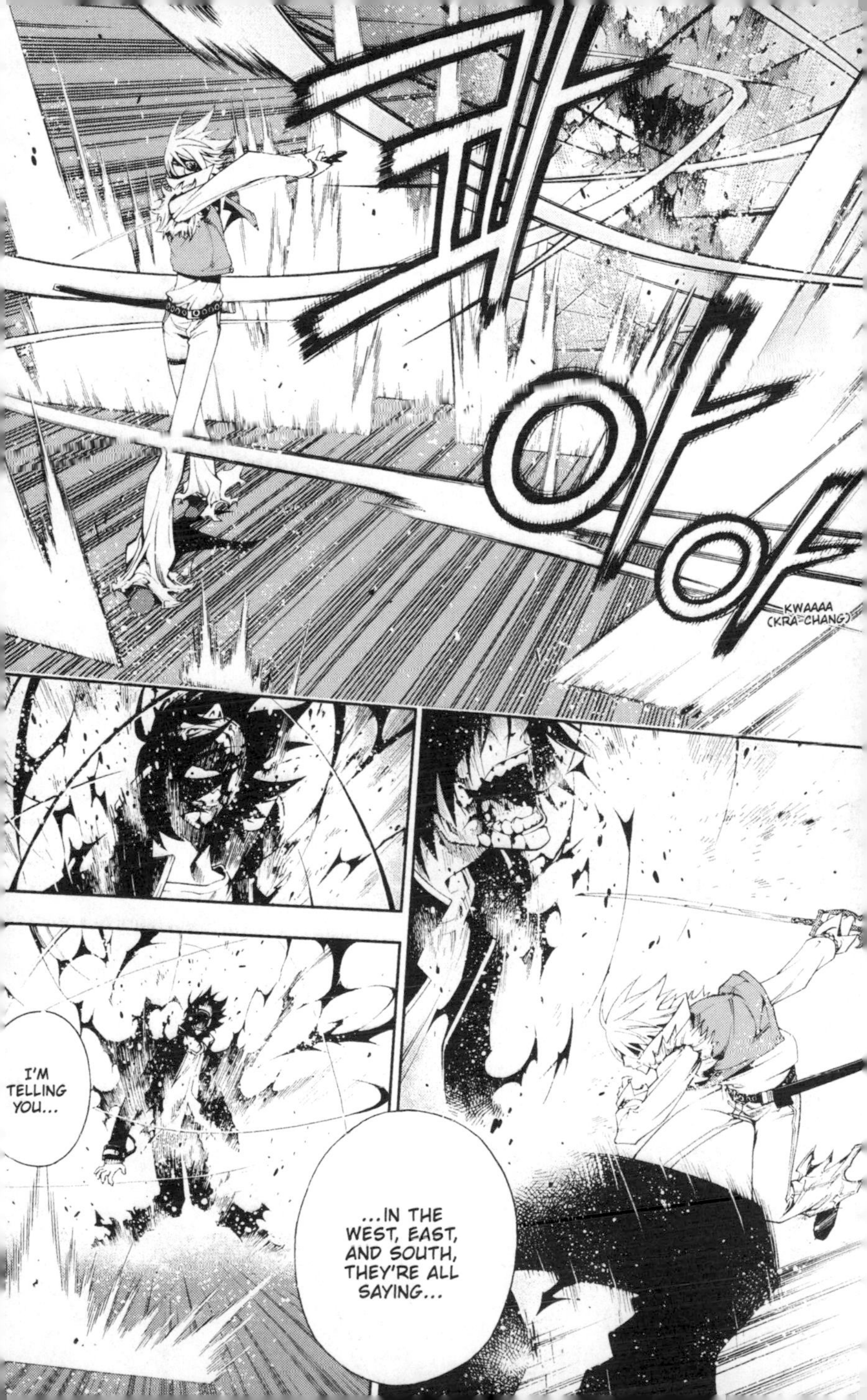
KWAAAA
(KRA-CHANG)
I'M TELLING YOU...
...IN THE WEST, EAST, AND SOUTH, THEY'RE ALL SAYING...

...THAT THE STRONGEST "SA-SHIN" RESIDES IN THE NORTH DISTRICT—!!
CHWARARAK (SKRAAAAA)
CHUD

푸우욱
POOK (STAB)
콰당
KWADANG (BUMP)
THE NAME JACK FROST IS...
...THE GREATEST TREASURE IN AMITYVILLE!
스우우우...
SHUUUU (WHOOSH)

...AM AVID, A BLOOD PIRATE WHO JUST LOVES TO HUNT...
AND I...
...TREASU–

ZZRIT ZZRIT
(BZZT BZZT)
TA-
(WH-)
-AK
(-ACK)

KAARRGH—!!
...
JILGUNG (MUNCH)
JILGUNG
≈SPIT≈
톡
TOK (THUMP)
부르르...
BURRRR (SHUDDER)
THIS IS GREAT.
...!
PIT (FFT)
PIT
SHIIIII (WHOOSH)

HEH-HEH-HEH... FINALLY, A GOOD, NEW STUDENT IN AMITYVILLE...
쉬리리리...
SHIRIRIRI (WHOOSH)
...YOU CAN MAKE ME TASTE THE JOY OF PAIN AGAIN...
H-HIS CLOAK... HEALS HIS BODY?!
WELL...
쉬이이...
SHIIII (SHLOOP)
솨아아아아...
SHWAAAAA (SWISH)

!
TOOK (TAK)
WHICK (THROW)
THANKS SO MUCH FOR YOUR GIFT TO YOUR "SUNBEI."
TO REPAY YOU...
...LET ME GRANT YOU THE GRANDEST DEATH EVER, LOVELY "HOOBEI"!

HA...
HA-HA-HA...!
SHU (CHOO) SHU SHU SHU
KOFF!
CRIPES ...!
FEEL! ENJOY!
KHA HA HA HA HA!!!

...THE DEATH FROM JACK!!

UH-OH...
저벅
EBUK
TAP)
저벅
JEBUK
저벅
JEBUK
저벅
JEBUK
JEBUK
저벅
JEBUK
저벅
WHAT THE HELL IS THAT?!
I'M
IGHTENED.
IST SHOW
OURSELF,
LREADY!
SSS (SHUFFLE)
스으
AIEEE!
콰직
KHWAJIK (CRASH)
EHHHH? WHY'S THE MIRROR IMAGE'S HEAD OUT HERE?
H-HANSEN!
I SHOULD JUST TAKE THIS AND HEAD BACK TO THE WEST DISTRICT!
OH, DAMN! HE CUT MY HEAD OFF IN THE FIRST PLACE!
바둥
바둥
BADUNG (SQUIRM) BADUNG

FEAR NOT. M'LADY TOLD ME TO GUARD YOU.
WHAA—? HE'S THE PRINCE?
B-BUT, HE'S UGLY!
......
WHAT WE REALLY SHOULD WORRY ABOUT...
...IS THEM—AVID'S "MEALS"!!

WHAT WE REALLY SHOULD WORRY ABOUT...
HA!
......
...IS THEM— AVID'S "MEALS"!
JACK FROST
The Amityville
VIOLENCE 5.
GENIE AND HANSEN

IT'S BAD ENOUGH AVID SUCKED THE BLOOD AND LIFE OUT OF THEM...
HEY, NOW! CAREFUL WITH THE HEAD.
...BUT NOW THEY'VE TURNED INTO SOMETHING LESS THAN HUMAN! POOR SAPS.
THEY'VE ONLY GOT TWO PRIMAL URGES...
ABSOLUTE OBEDIENCE TO THE MASTER OF BLOOD, AVID!
AND THE INSATIABLE INSTINCT TO FEED ON FLESH!

FOR THESE "ZOMBIE MATES," WE'RE NEXT ON THE DINNER MENU!

타
TA (BANG)
탕
TANG
탕
TANG

BBAKACK
(PACHUK)
MUNCH ON THIS!
...?!
...!
ACK! WHAT THE HELL'S HE DOING?!
TITIKTIK
(TA-TAK-TAK)

PAPA (POP)
AIEEE~!
PANG (BLAM)
HOW DO YOU LIKE MY FISHING, MIRROR IMAGE?
...!
KWAK (YOINK)
DIE, ZOMBIE, DIE! I LOVE THIS FEELING! HA-HA!
TANG (BANG)
W-WHAA? IS HE USING ME AS BAIT?!
TANG

PAT (FFT)
I'M RELIEVING ALL MY STRESS FROM JACK! OH THANKS, MIRROR IMAGE!
KIRICK (CLICK)
...
!
PAAK (ZOOM)
SFX: CHULKEUK (CRACK)
HEY, NOW!
철컥!
GIMME A SECOND TO RELOAD, WILL YA?!
KWANG (CRASH)
TA (BANG)
TA
TANG

콰당
KWADANG (BUMP)
OOOF-.
...
ZZIRIT (TINGLE)
저릿
?
......
OH BOY. DID I GET CARRIED AWAY?
ESULRUNG (STROLL)
어슬렁
어슬렁
ESULRUNG
I-ISN'T THAT THE BODY OF THE MIRROR IMAGE?!
KEK!

D-DAMN IT!
철컥 철컥
CHULKEUK (CLICK)
CHULKEUK
I-IT'S EMPTY!
ACK! DO SOMETHING, MORON!
KE-KEK~!
파 파 팍
PA (FFT)
PA
PAK
왁
WHA- (BRI-)
악
-AK (-GHT)
THE LIGHTS?!

콰아아
KWAAAA- (KRA-)
쿠콰
KUKWA (KA-BLAM)
!
콰콰
KUKWA
두콱
TUKWAK (KA-POW)
...!

퍽퍽
PUPU-
(WHEE-)
퍽
-PUK
(-CHUK)
앙앙앙
-AAA
(-KWAM)
ARRGGHH! WHAT CRAZY FOOL—? WHO'S SHOOTING?!
콰앙앙앙
KWAAAAAA
(BOOM)
...!

SYSTEM RECOVERY AT 81%. DUAL GAUNTLET SLAY, ON.
SECURITY SYSTEM RECOVERY AT 72%. MAINSTREAM POWER, ON!
SHUUUU (VRRRRMMM)

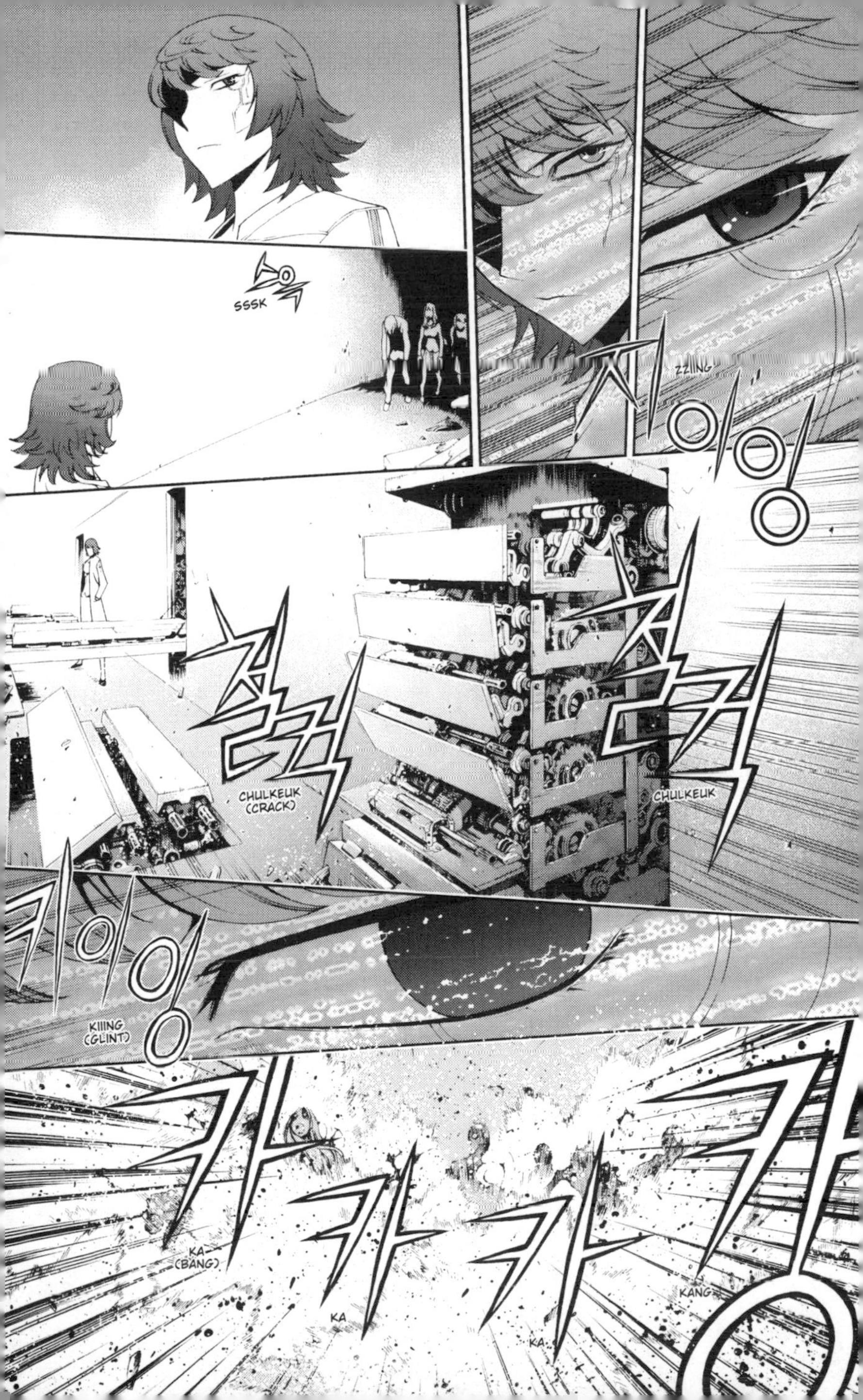

지이이잉
ZZIING
SSSK
철컥
CHULKEUK
철컥
CHULKEUK (CRACK)
키이잉
KIIING (GLINT)
카
KA (BANG)
카
KA
카
KA
캉
KANG

털썩
TULSUK (OOMP)
SYSTEM RECOVERY AT 99.89%! LESS THAN 0.23% SURVIVAL RATE.
지이잉
ZZIING
ALERT MODE SUSPENDED. RETURN TO THE NORMAL STREAM.
드르르르
DRRRR (CREAK)
SHHHHH
탁
TAK (TOK)
EVERYONE OKAY?
KAMJJACK (STARTLE)
깜짝!
......
SORRY I WAS LATE. I HAD A SLIGHT PROBLEM REGAINING CONSCIOUSNESS.
N-NOT AT ALL. P-PERFECT TIMING!
SHE'S A LITTLE SCARY...
I'M GLAD THAT JIN'S AWAKE. NOW SHE CAN PUT ME BACK TOGETHER...

THERE~. THE LINK HAS BEEN COMPLETED.
THE MIRROR IMAGE'S BLOOD IS A MIRACLE! MY WOUNDS ARE ALL HEALED!
......
YOU NEED SOME TIME TO HEAL...
WHINE~.
-DDUK (-CE)
I DON'T WANNA REST AGAIN! I'M THE GREAT MIRROR IMAGE...!
AH!
I-I'M SPEAKING?!
......
I CAN MOVE MY ARMS! MY LEGS! THIS ROCKS!

SHE MIGHT JUST CRACK A MARK.
IT HEALED EVEN FASTER THAN THE FIRST TIME!
YOU'RE SORTA LIKE A MONSTER, BUT IT'S COOL!
SHE'S EXCEEDING ALL EXPECTATIONS. QUITE AMAZING.
I MIGHT DO WHAT, NOW?
EH?
?
EEP!
깜짝
KAMJJACK (STARTLE)
WELL...
I'VE GOT SOME UNFINISHED BUSINESS...
훌러덩
HULODUNG (TAKE OFF)
WHAT'S THAT FOR?
WHOA-WHOA!
WE'VE GOT A MISUNDER-STANDING HERE!
I'M NO PERVERT!
W-WHAT THE HELL ARE YOU DOING, PERV?
I THOUGHT YOU LIKED GLASSES AND LONG HAIR?
PEUK (SMACK)
퍽
...
TAKE A LOOK AROUND.

....
?!
SSS
TH-THEY'RE NOT DEAD YET!
SSK
FOR ZOMBIES BITTEN BY VAMPIRES, ORDINARY GUNS DON'T WORK.
THE ONLY WAY TO GIVE THESE "MEALS" ETERNAL SLEEP...
...IS WITH A SILVER BULLET FROM THE GUN WITH A CROSS!

BACK TO WHERE YOU CAME FROM! HA! ASHES TO ASHES, DUST TO DUST!
TU (BANG)
TA
TANG
PUPUNG (KRA-CHUD)
TALKACK (CREAK)
PAAK (SHP)

PANG (SHP)
SHHK (SWISH)
TOO SLOW!
TANG
WOW...
HHHH WISH)
PANG (BANG)
AIEEE!
PA
PANG

UGH...
...
UGH
...
...
샤아아아아...
SHAAAAA (WHOOSH)
...
G-GONE, IN A PUFF OF SMOKE.
콰직
KWAJICK (BITE)
......
AND...
...THE ONLY WAY TO CURE A "MEAL" THAT WAS BITTEN NOT TOO LONG AGO...
NO! YOU'RE BITTEN!

CHIJIJI-
(SPLZZZZ-)
?!
-JICK
(-ZLE)
......!
KAARRGGHH!
SHUUUU
(SHHHHH)
BITLE
(REEL)
비틀
KWADANG
(BUMP)
SO, THIS GIRL IS...?
FIFTY-FIFTY CHANCE SHE'LL TURN BACK INTO A HUMAN, OR BE A ZOMBIE FOREVER.

HOW DO YOU KNOW ALL THIS?
WELL, YOU COULD SAY I LEARNED THE HARD WAY...
...FROM THE ONE WHO SAVED ME FROM THE CLUTCHES OF A VAMPIRE.
WELL, I'M NOT SURE, BUT HIS FAVORABILITY INCREASED BY 0.37%.
HE'S GOT A COMPLICATED PAST, EH? MAYBE HE'S NOT SO BAD AFTER ALL.
......
SFX: SOGUN (WHISPER) SOGUN
I'M HURT.
YOUR BLOOD CAN HEAL ME, MIRROR IMAGE!
THANKS~~~
YOUR BLOOD IS A WONDER DRUG!
OUCH! W-WHAT DID YOU DO THAT FOR?!
NEVER TOUCH A WOMAN WITHOUT ASKING, MORON!
...
?!
ARGH!

SHE MUST BE LOGGED INTO THE "ANCIENT ROCK."
I CAN SENSE MASTER JACK AND AVID'S FIGHT...
...I CANNOT ASCERTAIN HELMINA'S LOCATION.
OH, MS. HELMINA SHOULD'VE SEEN ME IN ACTION.
WHERE'RE AVID AND JACK?
...

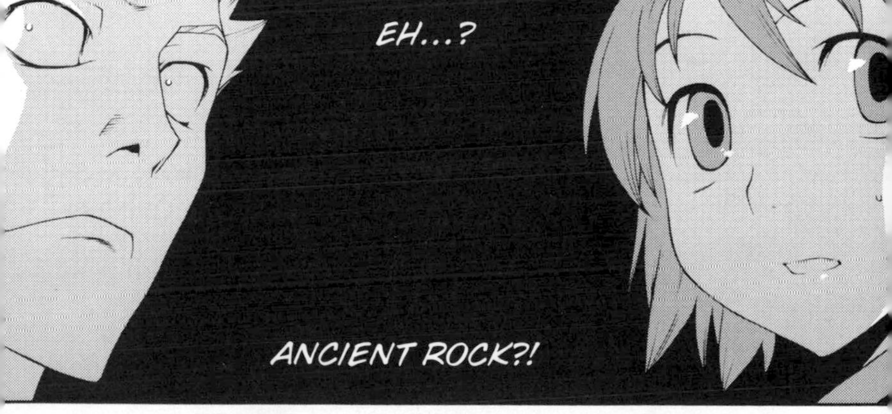
EH...?
ANCIENT ROCK?!

KUOHHHHHH
(VRRRMMM)

AVID...
AVID...
HMMM. NOT SURE WHY, HIS NAME STRIKES A CHORD IN ME.
BLOOD PIRATE AVID.
HE SEEMS POPULAR IN THE SOUTH DISTRICT.
멈칫
MUMCHIT (FREEZE)

νδ τηατ σωεετ χιτψ ωομ σηε
οντρολινγ μψ μινδ ανδ
ηεν ψου ρεαχη φ

AFTER THE THIRTEENTH DAY, HE CONFESSED...

...FATHER, I DRANK THE BLOOD OF A STRANGER!

ε ωαωεσ οφ τ ερε ισ δα
σομετηι ηαρε, ωε χ
ηατ σωε μαν, σηε μοω
ολινγ ψ μ ανδ μψ σουλ.
ψου εαχ ουτ φορ με, ψεαη, α
γετ νιγ φεωερ νιγητ φεωερ. Ω
τηατ νιγητ φεωερ, νιγητ φεωερ.

FEEL IT?!
SHU PAT (SHP SHP)
ZZTPANG (KRA-CHANG)
ENJOY IT?!
VIOLENCE 6. PROCLAMATION OF WAR
YOU WANT TO OFFER ME DEATH?!
KUNG (SWISH)
KWAAK (SMASH)

IS IT SO HARD TO BELIEVE?
SOONER OR LATER, YOU'LL SEE...
...THE MOST HORRIFYING DEATH!

YOU'LL MEET YOUR END IN THE MOST PERFECT SLAUGHTER!!
JACK FROST
The Amityville
VIOLENCE 6.
PROCLAMATION OF WAR

빠악
BBAAK (KRACK-KOW!)
SHUSHUSHU (WHOOSH)
QUOO (SHP)

TU TUK (CREAK)
CHAKANG (CLANG)
!
CHAKANG
OH~.
HIS CLOAK! WHAT THE HELL IS THAT?!

두웅
TUOONG
(THOOM)
KAK!
KULRUK
(COUGH)
...!

두콰콰콰
TUKWAKWAKWA
(CHA-THUD)
슈파앗
SHUPAAK
(PA-CHAK)

ONE EYE, ONE ARM. NOW YOU LOOK LIKE A REAL PIRATE.
WHAT...?
JURRRK (GURGLE)

TUK (BUMP)
CHANG (CLANG)
HE...
HEH HEH ...
HA!
KHA-HA-HA-HA-HA-HA!!
HEY, HOOBEI. YOU REALLY WANT A PATHETIC LAUGH TO BE YOUR LAST WORDS...
...BEFORE YOU DIE?
A-HA-HA-HA...
HA ...!
DDUK (STOP)
......
DEATH IS...

...THE FIRST STEP TOWARDS REBIRTH!
THE LONG JOURNEY OF CAUSALITY...
...IS CARRIED OUT BY THE KARMA OF HUMANS, WHO ENDLESSLY TRAVERSE THE LIVING WORLD AND THE REALM OF THE DEAD THROUGH DEATH AND REBIRTH...
THERE ARE, HOWEVER, EXCEPTIONS TO THE RULE.
SOME HAVE SUCH POWERFUL KARMIC EFFECTS THAT THE REALM OF THE DEAD REJECTS THEM.
JUST LIKE...
...YOU AND ME.
CHUOK (THOK)
THESE REJECTED SOULS END UP IN A SCHOOL NAMED AMITYVILLE.

YOU'RE DRIVING ME CRAZY!
...YOU'RE THE WORST— BUT ALSO THE STRONGEST STUDENT I'VE EVER MET!
OF ALL OF THEM...
I WANT YOU MORE THAN THE MIRROR IMAGE!!
MY HEART INSISTS ON FEASTING ON YOUR BLOOD!!

!
LOOK AT THEM! MONSTERS!
I'M NOT WEAK! THEY'RE JUST FREAKISHLY STRONG!
I WAS A HEAD OF THE GUIDANCE DEPT.!
DU (BOOM)
DU
DU
DU
!
WOW~ AWESOME.
THEY'RE TOTALLY DESTROYING THE SCHOOL.
...
THOSE FREAKS ARE MAKING ME LOOK BAD!
I'M JUST NORMAL, RIGHT?!
DA (TAK) DA DA
KWAANG (WHEE-CHUK)

HEH HEH HEH!
탓!
TAT (SKIP)
EVEN WITH ONE ARM, YOU CAN STILL LAUGH!
......
PUEK (KA-POW)
TELL ME, DO YOU FIND THIS FUNNY?!

팡
PANG (WHAM)
쿨럭
KULRUK (COUGH)
I-IS T-THIS...
...H-HOW I-I...
콰당
KWADANG (SLUMP)

UG...
...UGH!
파르르...
RRRR
EMBLE)
SFX: KOLRUK (COUGH) KOLRUK
...!
BUDLE (SHUDDER) BUDLE
DO YOU WANT MY BLOOD THAT BADLY?
HERE, THEN! FILL YOUR EMPTY VEINS WITH MY BLOOD...
...YOU LEECH!
H-HEY, WHOA!!
WHAT THE HELL IS HE DOING?

NOW I EVEN HATE MYSELF...
꾸물 꾸물
KUMUL (WRIGGLE) KUMUL
HEH-HEH...
I CAN'T TAKE IT ANYMORE...
!
......
...TO INJURY BY ATTACKING A VAMPIRE'S PRIDE?
YOU'RE ADDING INSULT...
NOT THAT I'M COMPLAINING. I'LL TAKE YOUR BLOOD!
I TOO HAVE A GIFT FOR YOU!
비틀
BITLE (STAGGER)
......

KWA- (BI-)
-AK (-TE)
!!
THAT STUPID IDIOT!
......!
!
HE IS NOW CONTROLLED BY THAT WHICH SUCKED HIS BLOOD!
CON-TROLLED BY THAT WHICH SUCKED HIS BLOOD?!
......!
SSK (FWIP)
YES, MA'AM! WHERE HAVE YOU BEEN?!
EXPLAIN.

THAT'S WHY ALL THOSE ZOMBIE MATES WE FOUGHT SERVE AVID!
VAMPIRES RULE THEIR VICTIMS WITH FEAR.
HE'S THEIR BLOOD MASTER. BECAUSE OF THIS INESCAPABLE FEAR, THEY LOSE POWER OVER THEIR BODIES AND MINDS!
JACK WALKED STRAIGHT INTO HELL ON HIS OWN!
...!
HE'S GONE TOO FAR.
!
GULP...
GULP.
GULP...

샤아 아아...
SHAAA (WHOOSH)
YOU ...!!
WHO ...?!
TO US ...!!
A-ARE Y-YOU GUYS...?
...
JA...
JACK...
JACK FROST ...!

HA~.

IT'S FUN.

THIS IS FUN.

CHWAAK (SWARM)

YOU DID THIS TO US...!!

NOW IT'S YOUR TURN!

THE PAIN!! THE PAIN!!

KWA (THWAP)

KWA

KWAK

IT HURTS ...!
IT REALLY HURTS ...!!
...!

DO YOU FEEL IT? ENJOY IT?!
THE VERY FEAR THAT LIVES WITHIN YOU?!
FOOL!
NOT SO STRONG NOW, EH, TOUGH GUY? YOU'RE TRAPPED!
HE'S IN DANGER. HE'S NOT RESPONDING TO ATTACKS.
HEY, MA'AM. JACK IS DYING.
NOT THAT I CARE.
......
AND YOU KNOW VERY WELL WHAT DEATH MEANS IN AMITYVILLE.

JIN.
CAN YOU BROADCAST THIS TO ALL THE DISTRICTS IN AMITYVILLE?
EH?
YES.
Hello, citizens of Amityville.
It is I, Helmina, head of North District.

To all the top students in the West, East, and South Districts!
HUH?
?
Are you tired of boring school life?
WHAT THE —?
THEY HACKED OUR BROADCAST SYSTEM!
...!
I CAN'T STOP THEM!
...!
Isn't the boredom of everyday monotony worse than death?!

WELL, IT'S YOUR LUCKY DAY...
second
MONITORRING NOW
volume testing.
...I HAVE THE ANSWER TO THIS TEDIUM!
BEH~
second
HI~.
MONITORRING NOW

We've all been expelled to Amityville, and we can never leave.
Both the world of the living and land of the dead rejected us.
There is no past life, no rebirth. This is the final destination for those who have already died.
THERE IS ONE OF US WHO IS CLOSE TO THE END...
...JACK FROST!
...JACK...
VIOLENCE 7. JACK'S DEATH

......
WHAT ...?!
IS THAT JACK... FROST?!
...JACK FROST!
YES. AS YOU ALL KNOW, HE IS THE STRONGEST IN THE NORTH DISTRICT.

I THOUGHT HE NEVER LOSES!
...
WHY IS SHE BROADCASTING THIS TO THE WHOLE SCHOOL...?
I-IS HE REALLY DYING?
SO LET'S FIND OUT...
...WHAT DEATH IS LIKE IN THIS FINAL DESTINATION...
THE TERMINATION OF THE LAW OF CAUSALITY!!
COMPLETE ERASURE FROM ALL WORLDS!

SHU (SHP)
IT'S OVER, JACK FROST!
WATCH...
PAAA (WHOOSH)
...THE DEATH OF JACK!!!
YOUR FEAR WILL BE THE DEATH OF YOU!

...!
KAARRGH!
THE PAIN!!

UN-LESS...
...YOU DIE.
HEH HEH ....!
KWA- (WHEE-)
...!
-AK (-CHUK)
W-WE WON'T DISAPPEAR!
I...
WE'LL BE WITH YOU FOREVER!!

DEATH...!
SURROUNDING HIS BODY LIKE A CLOAK... IS THAT...?!
...!
I- IT'S ...!
!!

CAN YOU FEEL IT...?!
...THE TEMPTATION OF DEATH SQUEEZING YOUR HEART?!
HEH HEH HEH...
FEAR IS...
...JUST AN ILLUSION FROM THOSE WHO FEAR DEATH.
NOTHING CAN DEFEAT ME, NOT FEAR NOR DEATH!
AND DON'T YOU FORGET THAT...

...!!
CHWAAK (SHWOOSH)
...THAT JACK FROST IS DEATH INCARNATE!!
FOR THE GRANDEST DEATH SCENE EVER...
...COME TO THE NORTH DISTRICT !!
WARRIORS OF AMITYVILLE! DO YOU WANT A MEMORABLE DEATH?!

Get killed by Jack Frost!!
...!
THAT'S ...
...JACK FROST.
WHAT THE HELL IS THAT BASTARD?

STRONGER THAN AVID, IS HE?
THEN THAT'S WHERE I'M HEADED. RIGHT?
HOW DARE YOU, HELMINA.
HOW COULD I RESIST SUCH A WONDERFUL PROCLAMATION?

HA...HA... I FOUGHT DEATH INCARNATE!
YOU'RE LUCKY TO BE ALIVE.
JU...
JUDA GE BLEED!
CHUAAAAAK (SHHHHHK
BEAUTIFUL, JACK! YOUR BODY, YOUR SOUL!
CHT- (POP)
-PANG (OUT)
I FELL IN LOVE WITH YOUR STRENGTH!
I'LL BE BACK TO GET YOU...
...
A WING CAME OUT..
...FROM THE EYE PATCH?
...MY PRECIOUS TREASURE!!
PUDEDEK (FLUTTER)
푸드득
KHA HA HA ...!

......
AVID, I'LL RIP THOSE FEATHERS OUT MYSELF NEXT TIME!
...
H!

...
IT'S ALL SO FAMILIAR...?
BLOOD...IS BEAUTIFUL.
NOH-A JOO...
...I MEAN, MIRROR IMAGE.
YOU'VE MADE AMITYVILLE'S COMPASS OF CAUSALITY MOVE ONCE AGAIN!!
......
SNOW...
...AND BLOOD?

AFTER THE THIRTEENTH DAY, HE CONFESSES. FATHER, I DRANK THE BLOOD OF A STRANGER!
JACK AND AVID'S BATTLE WAS JUST THE BEGINNING.
OH, I ALMOST FORGOT!
I MUST TELL YOU HOW I VALIANTLY PROTECTED THE MIRROR IMAGE!
AH! SON! MY SONS! YOU HAVE TASTED THE OTHER WORLD.
WHEN THE COMPASS NEEDLE SIGNALS THE END OF THEIR KARMA...
REMEMBER HOW GREAT I WAS? YO, WHAT'S THE MATTER?
...
YOU WILL BE SENT TO THE DARK SIDE, NEVER TO RETURN.
...THE LAST LEGEND OF AMITYVILLE WILL END!

ONLY THE LAST STRANGER CAN BRING US SALVATION!!
THE DEAD OF AMITYVILLE WILL RISE AGAIN!
AH...
I REMEMBER...
...JACK FROST!

IT'S MY DAD'S DOLL— THE DOLL THAT WILL PROTECT ME!!
TO BE CONTINUED IN VOLUME 2!!

TRANSLATION NOTES

Page 108
Sa-Shin: The Korean word that can be roughly translated into "God of Death." It is the equivalent of shinigami in Japanese.

Page 114
Sunbei: The Korean word for upperclassman. It is the equivalent of *senpai* in Japanese.

Hoobei: The Korean word for underclassman. It is the equivalent of *kohai* in Japanese.

JACK FROST, VOL. 2 PREVIEW

THE PILLAR OF SOLOMON, WHERE THE DEADLIEST PRISONERS ARE HELD!

THOSE WHO PROTECT IT AND THOSE TRYING TO BREAK IT ARE AT WAR!

THE EXCITEMENT CONTINUES...

...AS THE MIGHTY WARRIORS OF AMITYVILLE GATHER TOGETHER!

READ ALL ABOUT IT IN JACK FROST, VOLUME 2!

JACK FROST ①

JINHO KO

Translation: JiEun Park
English Adaptation: Arthur Dela Cruz

Lettering: Jose Macasocol Jr.

Yen Press
Hachette Book Group
237 Park Avenue, New York, NY 10017

Visit our Web sites at www.HachetteBookGroup.com and www.YenPress.com.

Yen Press is an imprint of Hachette Book Group, Inc.
The Yen Press name and logo are trademarks of Hachette Book Group, Inc.

First Yen Press Edition: May 2009

ISBN-13: 978-0-7595-2954-0

10 9 8 7 6 5 4 3 2 1

BVG

Printed in the United States of America